Inside Machines
Helicopters

David West

Published in 2018 by **Windmill Books**,
an imprint of Rosen Publishing
29 East 21st Street, New York, NY 10010

Copyright © 2018 David West Children's Books

All rights reserved. No part of this book may be reproduced in any form
without permission in writing from the publisher, except by a reviewer.

Designed and illustrated David West

Cataloging-in-Publication Data
Names: West, David.
Title: Helicopters / David West.
Description: New York : Windmill Books, 2018. | Series: Inside machines | Includes index.
Identifiers: ISBN 9781499483314 (pbk.) | ISBN 9781499483253 (library bound) | ISBN 9781499483130 (6 pack)
Subjects: LCSH: Helicopters–Juvenile literature.
Classification: LCC TL716.2 W47 2018 | DDC 629.133'352–dc23

Manufactured in the United States of America
CPSIA Compliance Information: Batch BS17WM: For Further Information contact Rosen Publishing, New York, New York at 1-800-237-9932

Contents

Helicopter 4

Inside a Helicopter 6

Chinook 8

Inside a Chinook 10

Helicopter gunship 12

Inside a Helicopter gunship 14

NOTAR helicopter 16

Inside a NOTAR helicopter 18

Stealth helicopter 20

Inside a Stealth helicopter 22

Glossary and Index 24

Helicopter

The simplest helicopters have one large main **rotor** with a smaller tail rotor at the back. Unlike planes, helicopters can hover. This means they do not need long runways to land and take off. They are used for many jobs such as farming, responding to emergencies, and reporting the news.

This small Hughes 300 helicopter is spraying crops. It has room for two people and is often used to train helicopter pilots.

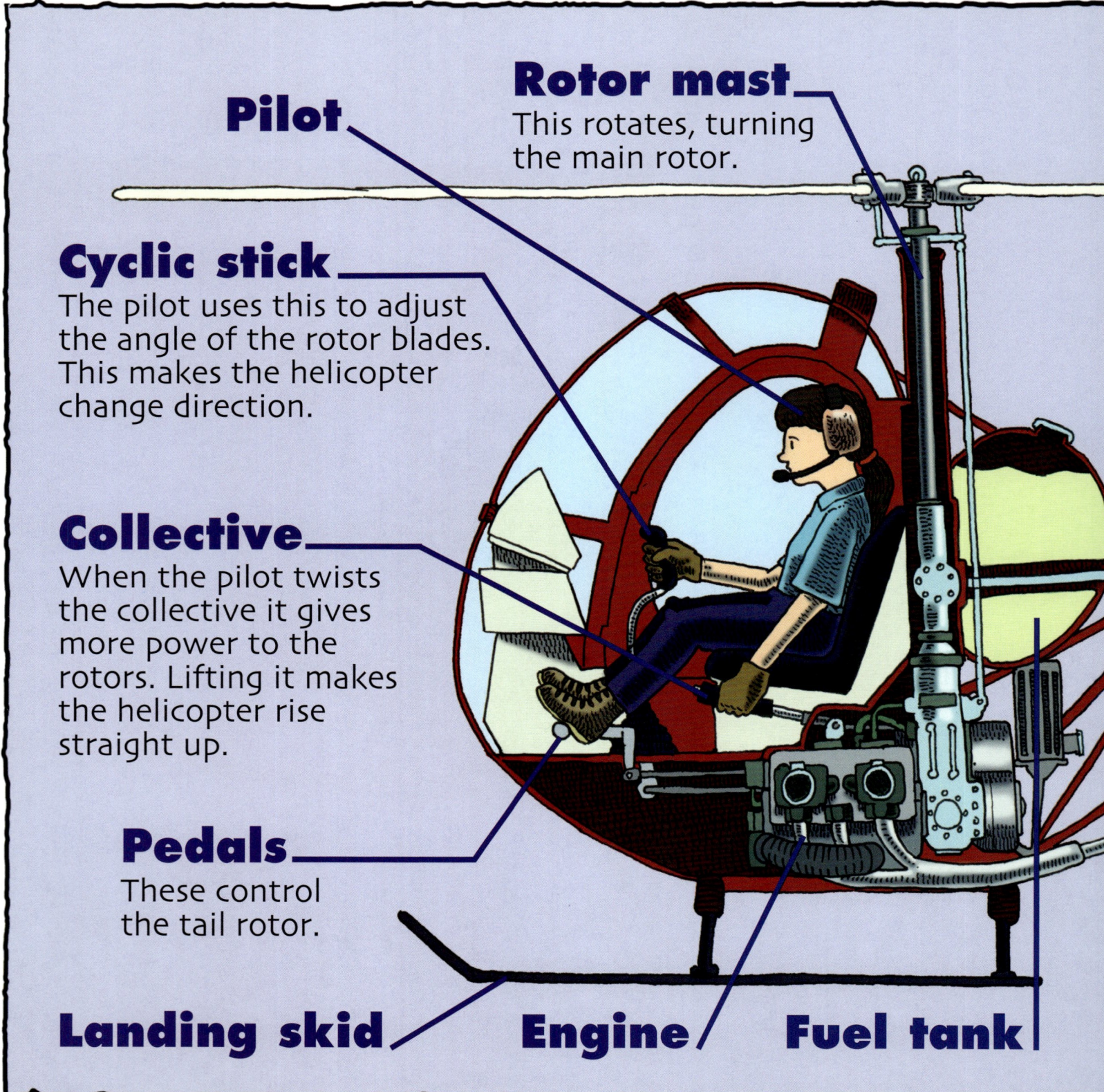

Inside a Helicopter

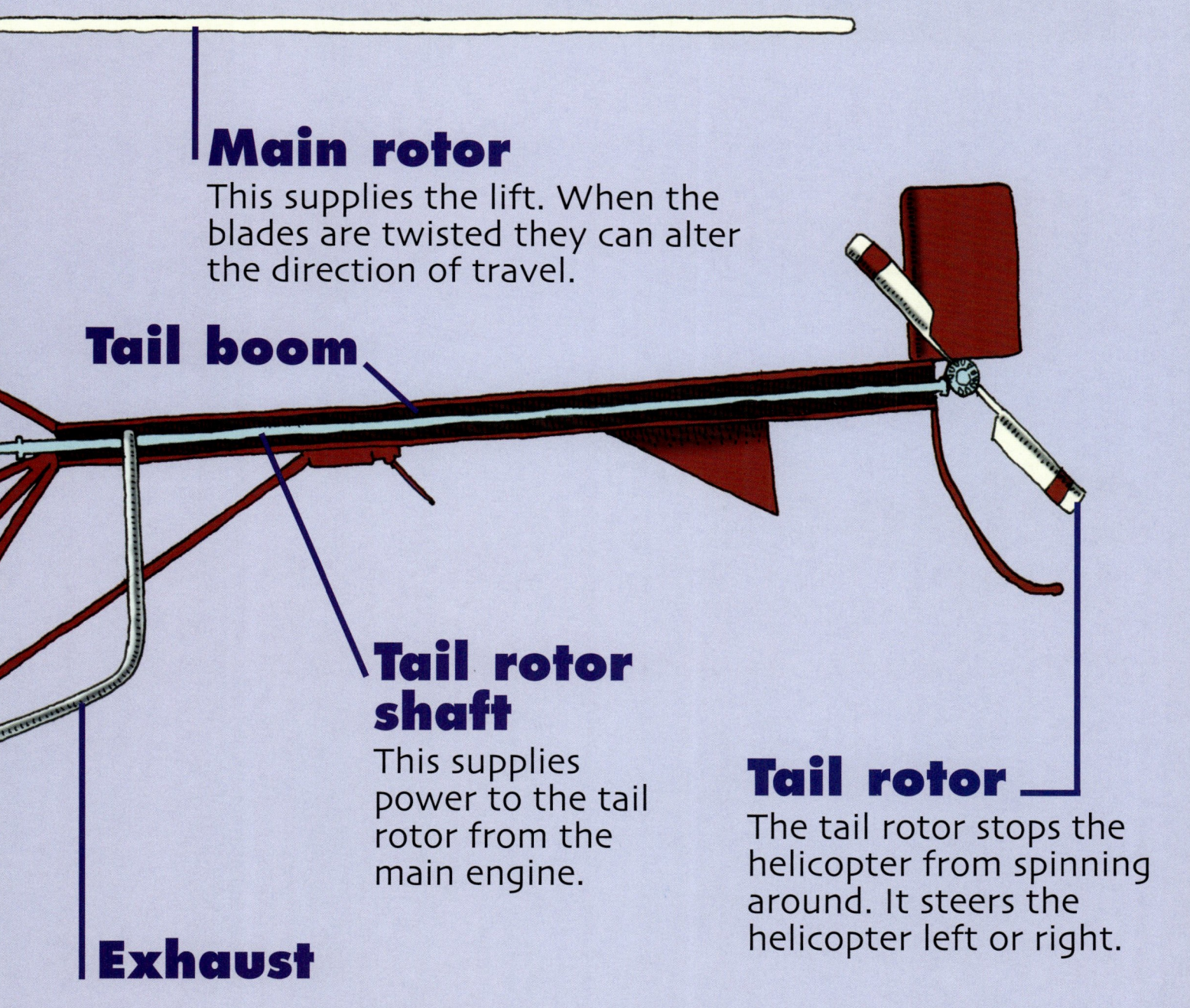

Main rotor
This supplies the lift. When the blades are twisted they can alter the direction of travel.

Tail boom

Tail rotor shaft
This supplies power to the tail rotor from the main engine.

Tail rotor
The tail rotor stops the helicopter from spinning around. It steers the helicopter left or right.

Exhaust

The Chinook is a heavy-lift helicopter. It is mainly used for carrying troops, artillery guns, and supplies to the battlefield.

Chinook

This large helicopter has two sets of main rotors. They rotate in different directions from each other. This stops the helicopter from twisting around just as the tail rotor does on a single rotor helicopter. The Chinook has two powerful **turboshaft** engines at the back. These supply the power to the back and front rotors.

Inside a Chinook

Cabin
The cabin can carry 59 passengers or a combined load of passengers and cargo.

Front rotor

Cockpit
The helicopter is flown by the pilot and copilot from the cockpit.

Pilot

Electronics

Fuel tank

Landing gear

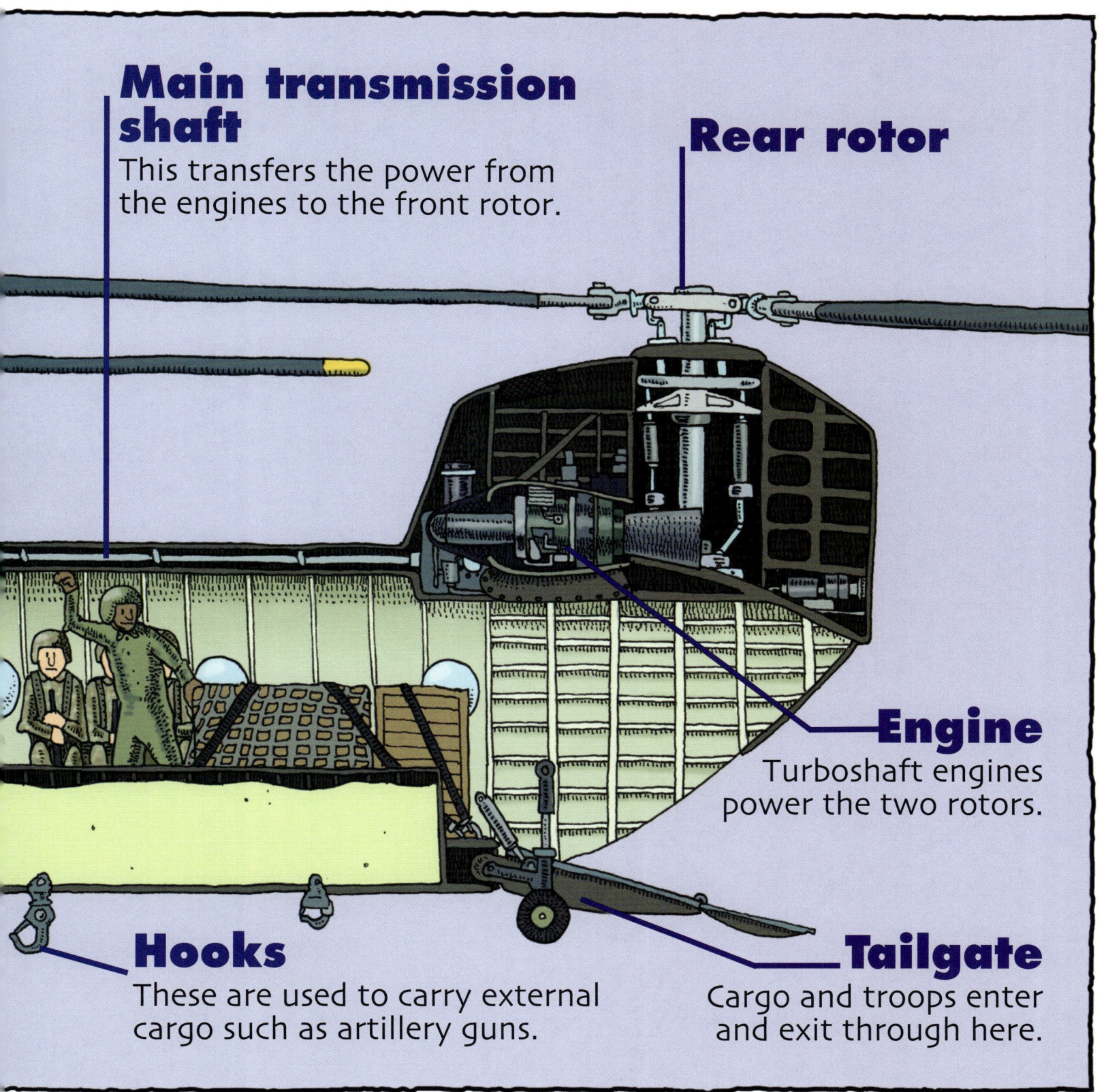

Helicopter gunship

This large, heavily-armed helicopter gunship bristles with weapons. It is carrying machine guns, rockets, cannons, and missiles. These are fired by the weapons officer in the front cockpit. The pilot sits behind in a separate cockpit. The gunship is also heavily armored. The fuselage, cockpit, and rotor head can withstand being hit by small cannon fire.

This Mil Mi-24 is often called the "flying tank" by its Russian pilots. It carries eight combat troops in the cabin behind the cockpits.

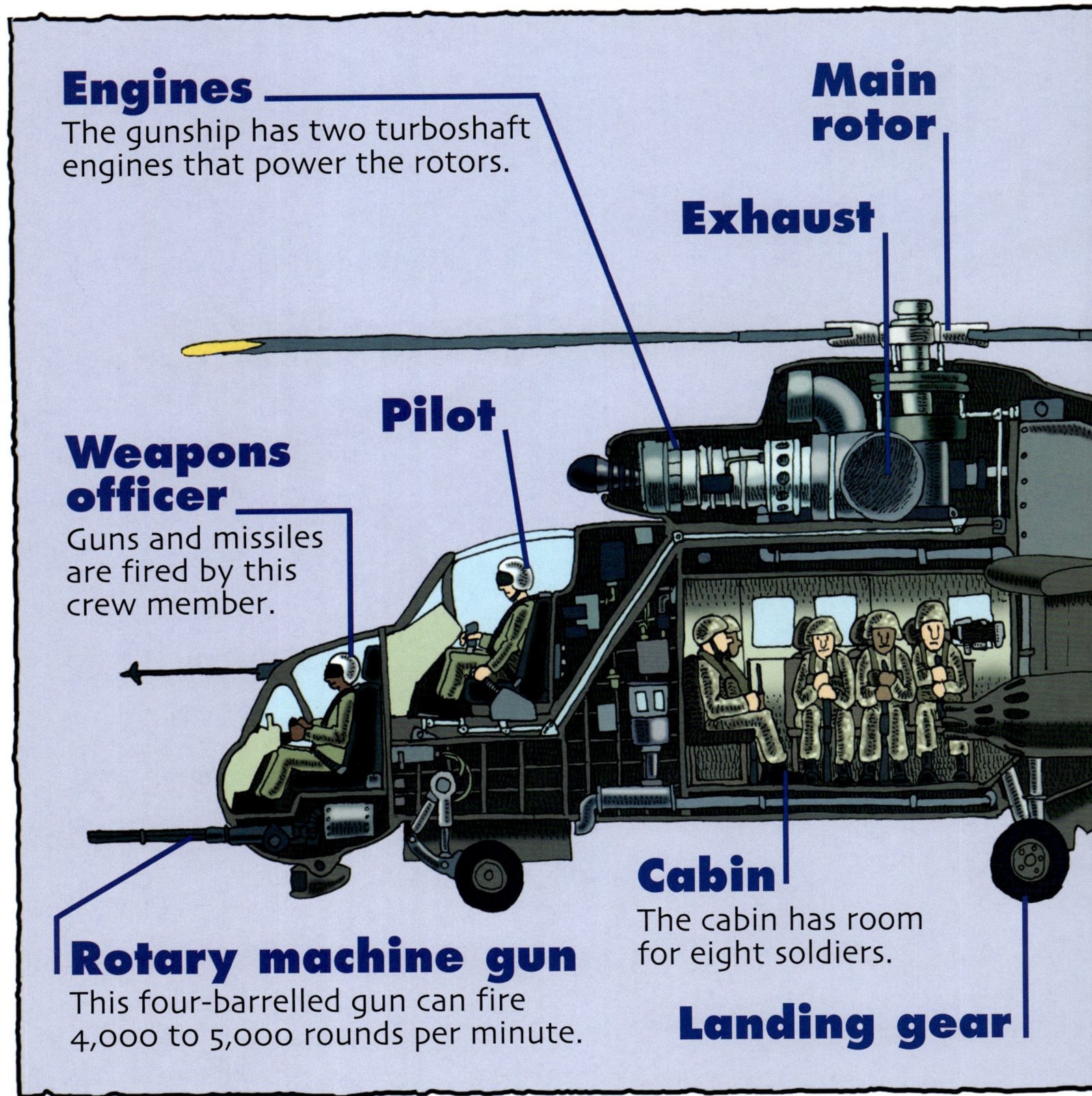

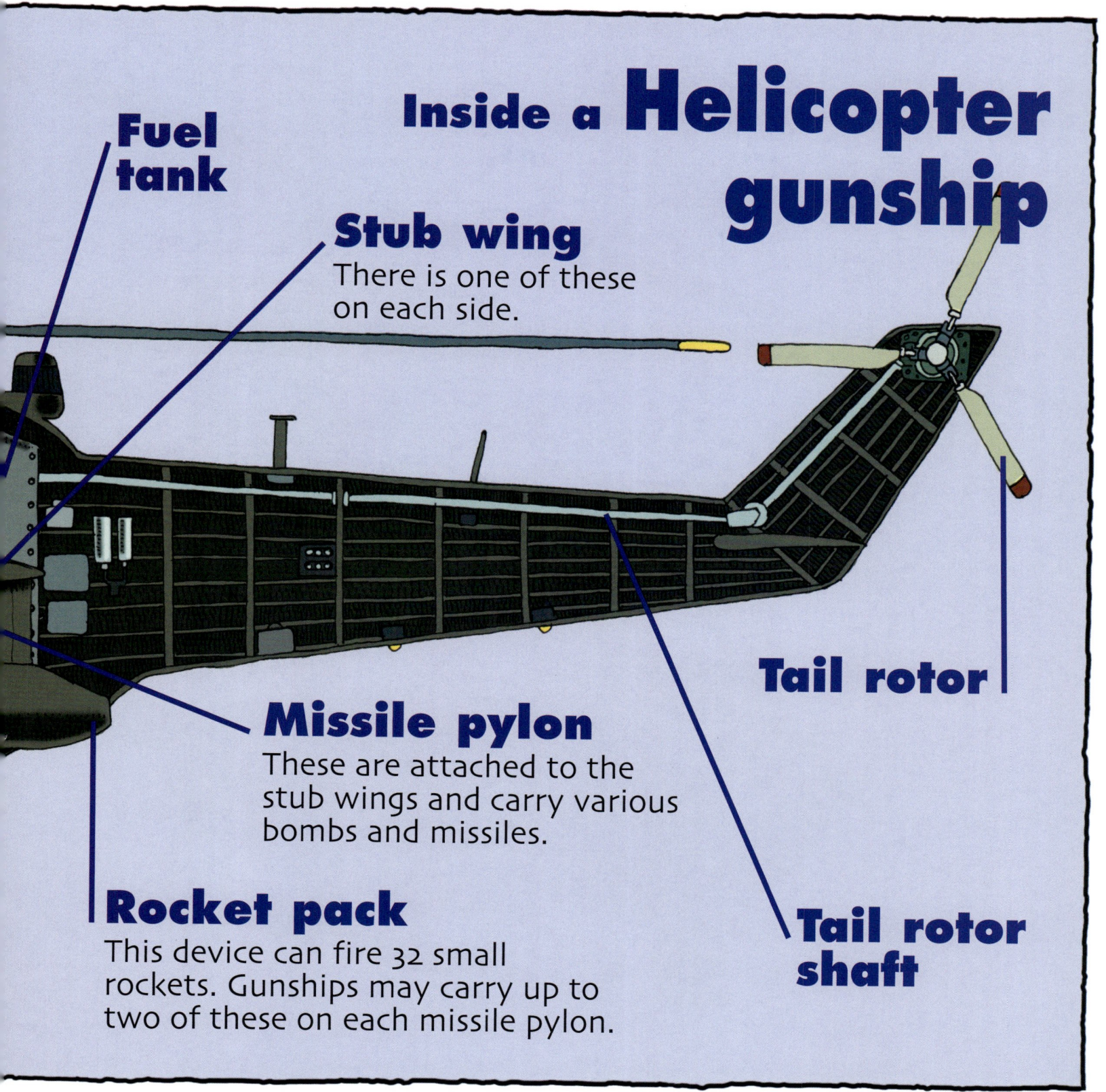

Inside a Helicopter gunship

Fuel tank

Stub wing
There is one of these on each side.

Tail rotor

Missile pylon
These are attached to the stub wings and carry various bombs and missiles.

Tail rotor shaft

Rocket pack
This device can fire 32 small rockets. Gunships may carry up to two of these on each missile pylon.

This MD Explorer is used by the police. It has a pod attached to the front which houses two cameras. One is a daytime camera with a powerful zoom lens. The other uses **thermal imaging** to detect people hiding at night.

NOTAR helicopter

NOTAR stands for "NO TAil Rotar." This clever system uses a fan to push air out of gaps in the tail boom. It has the same effect as a tail rotor, stopping the helicopter from rotating in the opposite direction of the rotor. It is quieter and safer than helicopters with tail rotors.

Inside a NOTAR helicopter

Tail fin

Air intake

Exhaust

Tail boom

Air slots

Fan
A fan in the tail boom is driven by the engine. It sucks in air through intakes and thrusts it out through slots. This stops the helicopter from rotating.

Vented drum
The drum at the end rotates, pushing air out left or right to make the helicopter face either way. This has the same purpose as a tail rotor.

Luggage area

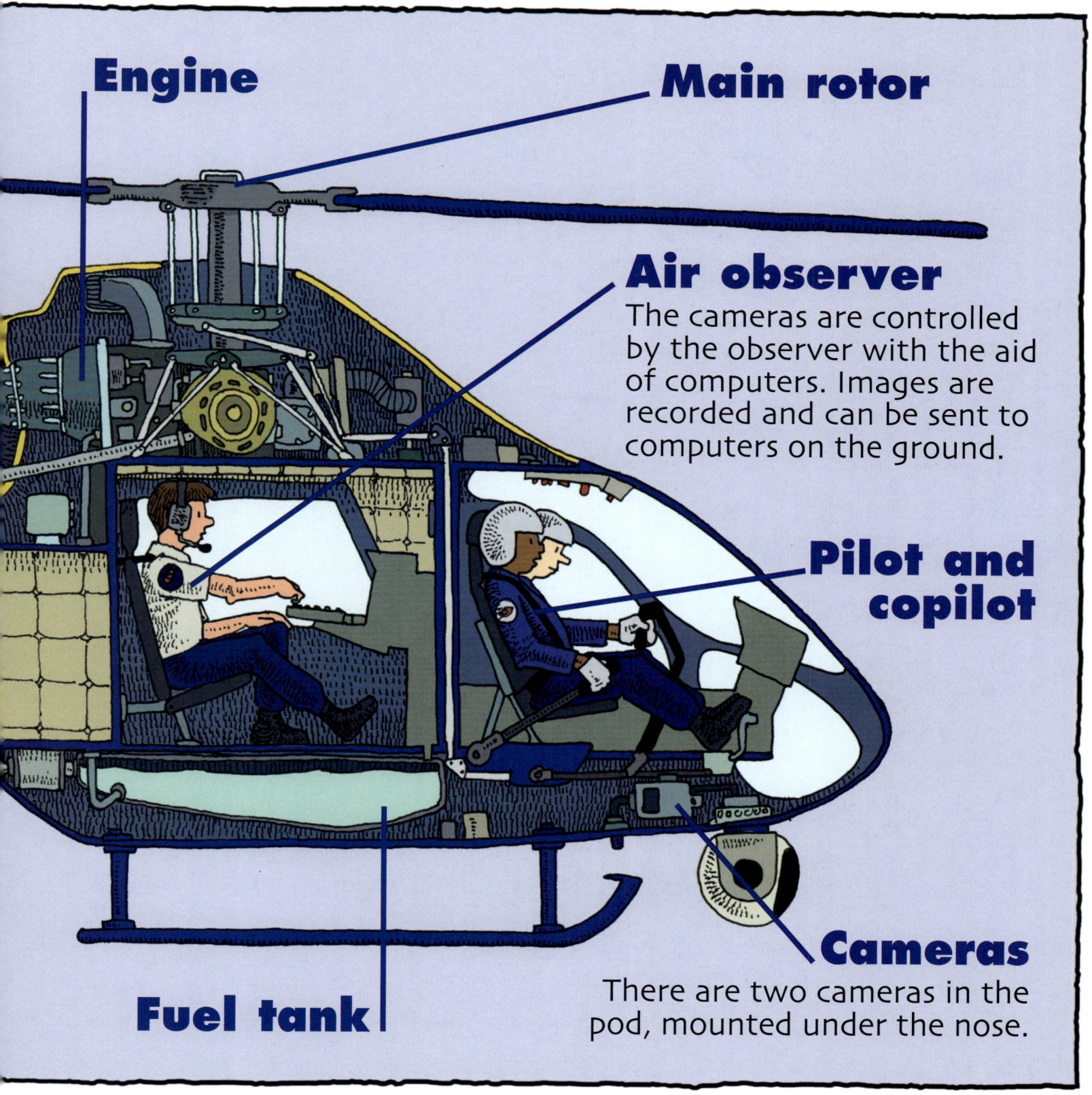

This Boeing-Sikorsky RAH-66 Comanche was an advanced five-blade, armed reconnaissance and attack helicopter designed for the United States Army. Only two test helicopters were made before the program was canceled.

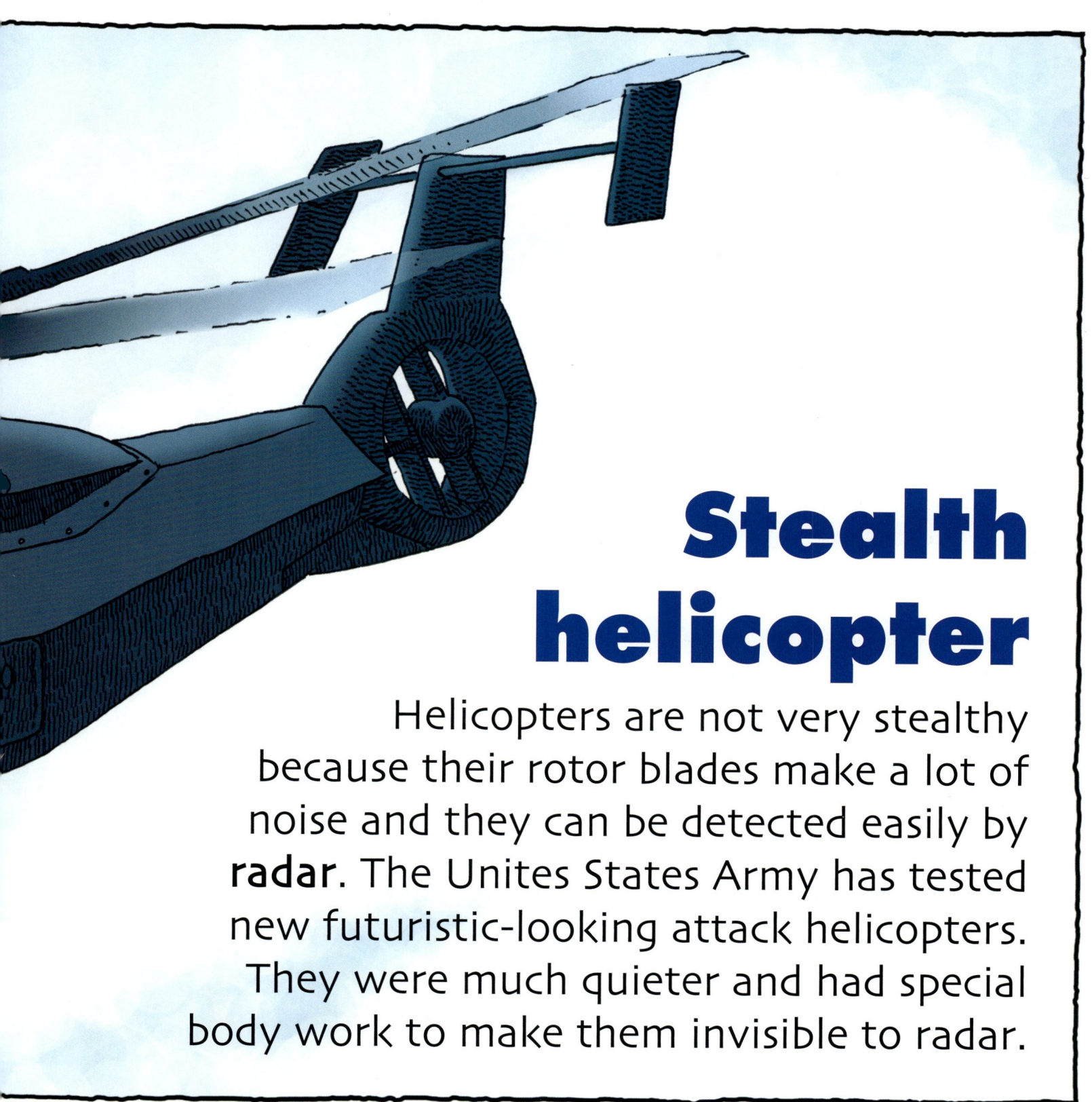

Stealth helicopter

Helicopters are not very stealthy because their rotor blades make a lot of noise and they can be detected easily by **radar**. The Unites States Army has tested new futuristic-looking attack helicopters. They were much quieter and had special body work to make them invisible to radar.

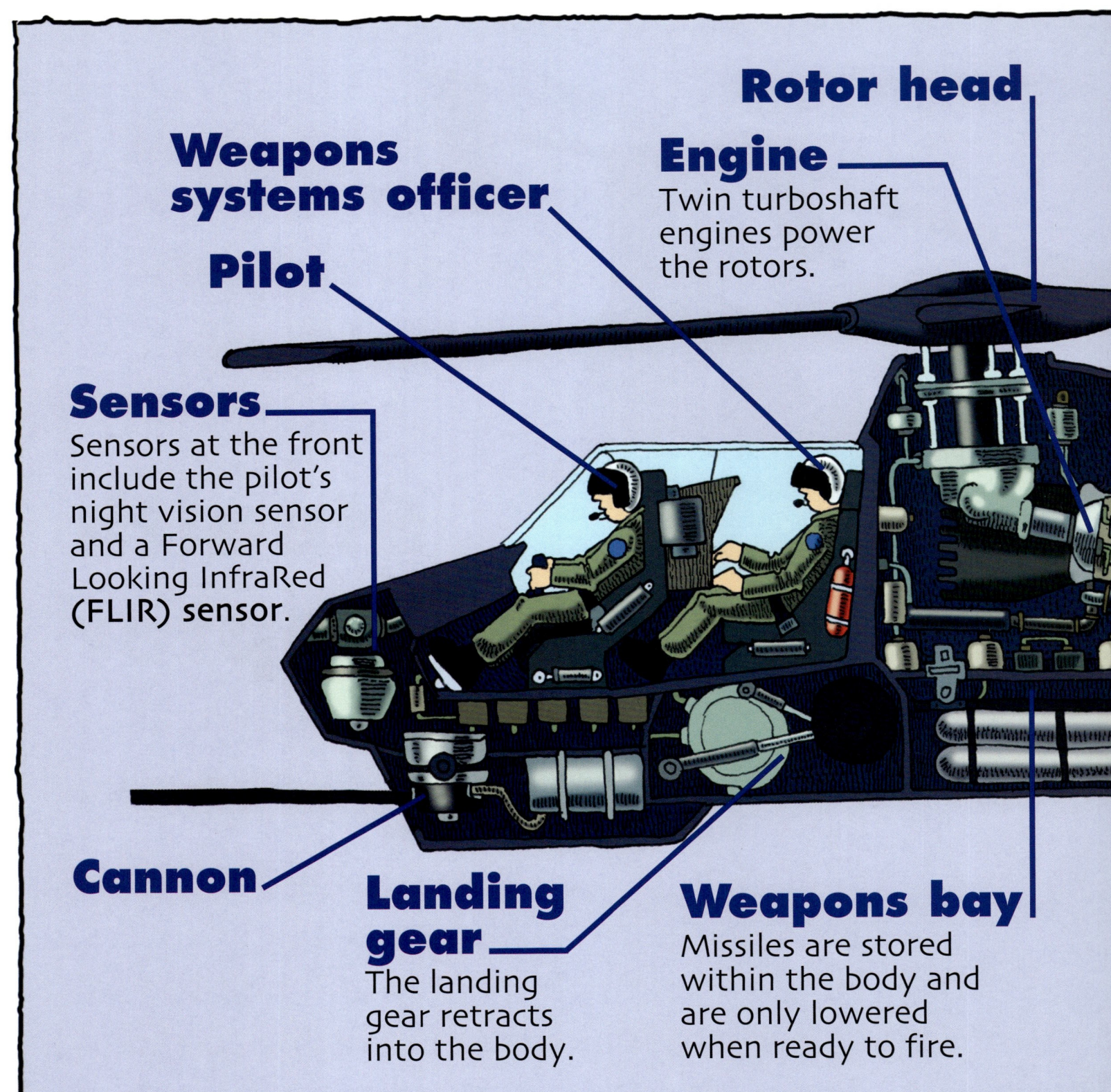

Inside a Stealth helicopter

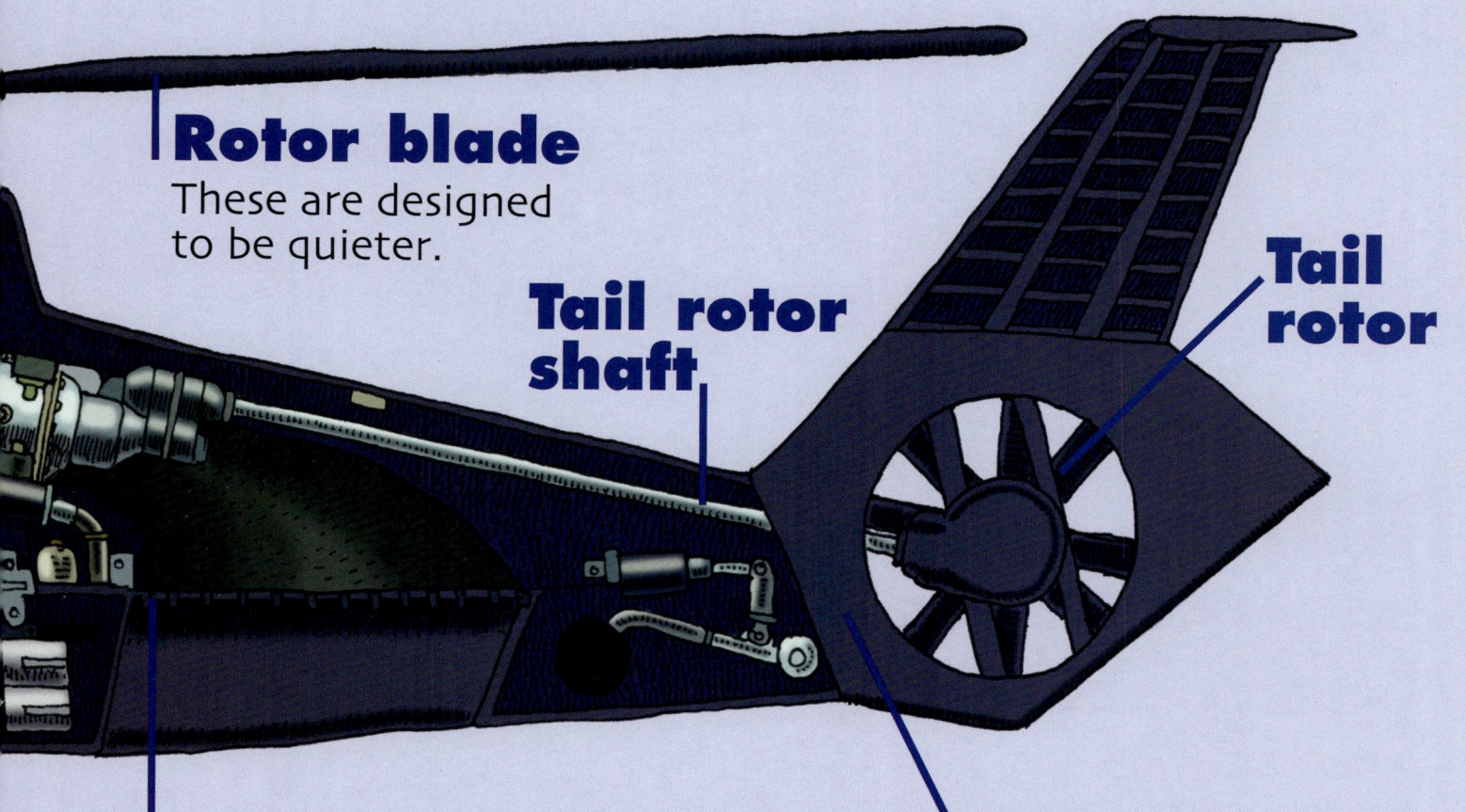

Rotor blade
These are designed to be quieter.

Tail rotor shaft

Tail rotor

Engine exhaust
The hot gases from the engine exit through grills along its tail. This makes them less likely to be picked up by enemy heat-seeking missiles.

Tail section
The tail section covers the tail rotor which muffles its noise.

Glossary

FLIR sensor
A camera that can detect things that give off heat, such as human bodies.

radar
A system that uses radio waves to detect objects and displays the objects' positions on a screen.

rotor
A rotating helicopter wing.

thermal imaging
The process of detecting things that give off heat.

turboshaft
An engine similar to a jet engine. Instead of producing thrust like a jet engine it powers a shaft.

Index

attack helicopter 20–23

Boeing-Sikorsky RAH-66 Comanche 20–23

camera 16, 19

Chinook 8–11

cockpit 10, 12

collective 6

cyclic stick 6

engine 7, 8, 11, 14, 18, 19, 22, 23

FLIR 22, 24

gunship 12–15

Hughes 300 4–7

MD Explorer 16–19

NOTAR 16–19

police 16

radar 21, 24

weapons 8, 11, 12, 14, 15, 22, 23